THE HOMESCHOO

Book of Centuries

This Book Belongs To:

A PORTABLE TIMELINE
FOR CHARLOTTE MASON AND
CLASSICAL EDUCATION STUDENTS

ANNA TRAVIS

The Homeschool History Book of Centuries
A Portable Timeline for Charlotte Mason and Classical Education Students
Rethink Schooling Series

©2016 Anna Travis

ISBN 13 : 978-1533118592
ISBN : 1533118590

Sweet Messy Faith
www.AnnaTravis.com

For the One who made me.

**If you enjoy this Book of Centuries,
please leave a review on Amazon.com.
It is a *huge* help to our family!**

A Note to Parents:

This Book of Centuries is divided into history eras. As you and your students move forward in time, you will find the eras have more pages for recording. There is one, continuous timeline running through the book, and it has lines to divide the decades and/or years. The years have intentionally been left off of those lines, so that your students can pen them in as they study a period. In our own family, I found that my children took ownership of their books better that way (and in the times when there are few specific dates to record, it gave them something to put down on paper)!

I hope this book is an affordable option for students and parents who are interested in chronicling their history studies. If you have any suggestions for the second edition, or requests for other home education materials, please contact me at www.AnnaTravis.com, where you can check out my Bible coloring journals, adult coloring books, and Christian Fantasy Adventure books.

Era	Time Covered
Prehistory	Dawn of Time – 3000 BC
The Ancients	3000 BC – 500 BC
Classical Civilizations	500 BC – 500 AD
The Middle Ages	500 AD – 1500 AD
Renaissance and Reformation	1500 AD – 1600 AD
Exploration And Colonization	1600 AD – 1750 AD
Industrial Revolution	1750 AD – 1900 AD
The Modern World	1900 AD – 2060 AD

Dear Fellow Time Traveler,

This book is your very own, portable timeline. Use it to jot down whatever you find most interesting and fascinating in your history studies.

The early periods (such as the Ancients and the Middle Ages) have only 2 pages for each century, while the Modern World has a new page for every five years. Hopefully this will give you enough room to record what you find fascinating about the era, but not leave you with great big empty spots during the times before Google!

Take your time and use your best hand-writing; you will want to add to your Book of Centuries for many years. Some people like to glue in pictures, while others draw. If you draw, do your best, but *enjoy* it! Do not stress about having to be perfect!

Here are some things you can record:
- Heroes (kings, conquerors, inventors, authors, you and your family)
- Villains (Hitler, Attila the Hun, etc.)
- Discoveries and Inventions
- Nations and Empires
- Wars and Battles
- Art and Music
- Religion

Happy exploring!

Pre-History

DAWN OF TIME TO —»

Pre-History

«— TO 3000BC

The Ancients

3000 BC to —»

The Ancients

«— to 2900 BC

The Ancients

2900 BC to —»

The Ancients

«— to 2800 BC

The Ancients

2800 BC to —»

The Ancients

«— to 2700 BC

The Ancients

2700 BC to —»

The Ancients

«— to 2600 BC

ANCIENTS

The Ancients

2600 BC to —»

The Ancients

«— to 2500 BC

The Ancients
2500 BC to —»

The Ancients
«— to 2400 BC

The Ancients

2400 BC to —»

The Ancients

«— to 2300 BC

The Ancients

2300 BC to —»

The Ancients
«— to 2200 BC

The Ancients

2200 BC to —»

The Ancients

«—— to 2100 BC

The Ancients

2100 BC to —»

The Ancients
«— to 2000 BC

The Ancients

2000 BC to —»

The Ancients
«— to 1900 BC

The Ancients

1900 BC to —»

The Ancients

«— to 1800 BC

The Ancients

1800 BC to —»

The Ancients

« — to 1700 BC

The Ancients

1700 BC to—»

The Ancients

«— to 1600 BC

The Ancients

1600 BC to —»

The Ancients

«— to 1500 BC

The Ancients

1500 BC to —»

The Ancients

«— to 1400 BC

The Ancients

1400 BC to —»

The Ancients

«— to 1300 BC

The Ancients

1300 BC to —»

The Ancients

«— to 1200 BC

The Ancients

1200 BC to —»

The Ancients

«— to 1100 BC

The Ancients

1100 BC to —»

The Ancients

«— to 1000 BC

The Ancients

1000 BC to —»

The Ancients

«— to 900 BC

The Ancients

900 BC to —»

The Ancients

«— to 800 BC

The Ancients

800 BC to —»

The Ancients

«— to 700 BC

The Ancients

700 BC to —»

The Ancients

«— to 600 BC

The Ancients

600 BC to —»

ANCIENTS

The Ancients

«— to 500 BC

Classical Civilizations

500 BC to —»

Classical Civilizations

«— to 400 BC

Classical Civilizations

400 BC to —»

CLASSICAL

Classical Civilizations
«— to 300 BC

Classical Civilizations

300 BC to —»

Classical Civilizations
«— to 200 BC

Classical Civilizations

200 BC to —»

Classical Civilizations

«— to 100 BC

Classical Civilizations

100 BC to —»

Classical Civilizations

«— to 0 AD

CLASSICAL

Classical Civilizations

0 AD to —»

Classical Civilizations

«— to 100 AD

Classical Civilizations

100 AD to —»

Classical Civilizations

«— to 200 AD

Classical Civilizations

200 AD to —»

CLASSICAL

Classical Civilizations

«—to 300 AD

Classical Civilizations

300 AD to —»

Classical Civilizations

«— to 400 AD

Classical Civilizations

400 AD to —»

Classical Civilizations

«— to 500 AD

The Middle Ages

500 AD to —»

The Middle Ages

«— to 600 AD

The Middle Ages

600 AD to —»

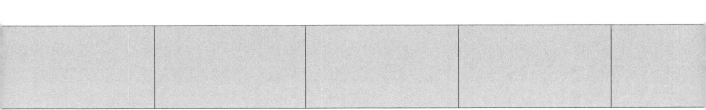

The Middle Ages

«— to 700 AD

The Middle Ages

700 AD to —»

MIDDLE AGES

The Middle Ages

«— to 800 AD

The Middle Ages

800 AD to —»

The Middle Ages

«— to 900 AD

The Middle Ages

900 AD to —»

The Middle Ages

《— to 1000 AD

The Middle Ages

1000 AD to —»

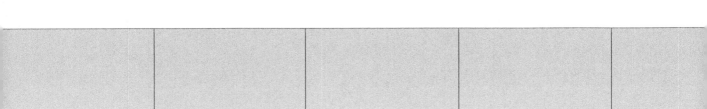

The Middle Ages

«— to 1100 AD

The Middle Ages

1100 AD to —»

The Middle Ages

«— to 1200 AD

MIDDLE AGES

The Middle Ages

1200 AD to —»

MIDDLE AGES

The Middle Ages

«— to 1300 AD

The Middle Ages

1300 AD to —»

The Middle Ages

«— to 1400 AD

The Middle Ages

1400 AD to —»

The Middle Ages

«— to 1500 AD

Renaissance & Reformation

1500 AD to —»

RENAISSANCE

Renaissance & Reformation

«— to 1550 AD

Renaissance & Reformation

1550 AD to —»

RENAISSANCE

Renaissance & Reformation

«— to 1600 AD

Exploration & Colonization

1600 AD to —»

Exploration & Colonization
«— to 1650 AD

Exploration & Colonization

1650 AD to —»

EXPLORATION

Exploration & Colonization

«— to 1700 AD

Exploration & Colonization

1700 AD to —»

Exploration & Colonization
«— to 1750 AD

EXPLORATION

Industrial Revolution

1750 AD to 1760 AD

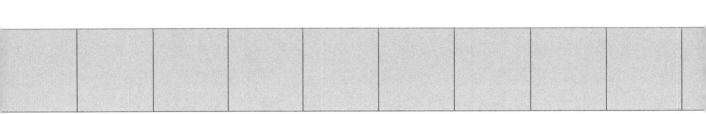

Industrial Revolution

1760 AD to 1770 AD

Industrial Revolution
1770 AD to 1780 AD

Industrial Revolution

1780 AD to 1790 AD

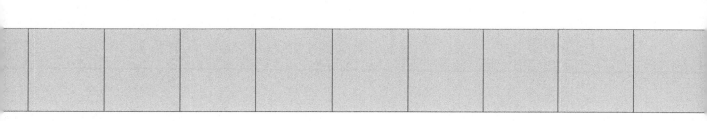

Industrial Revolution
1790 AD to 1800 AD

Industrial Revolution

1800 AD to 1810 AD

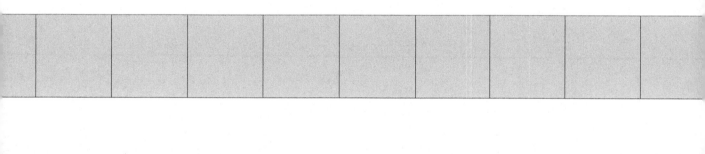

Industrial Revolution
1810 AD to 1820 AD

Industrial Revolution
1820 AD to 1830 AD

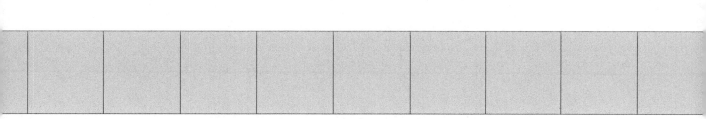

Industrial Revolution

1830 AD to 1840 AD

Industrial Revolution

1840 AD to 1850 AD

Industrial Revolution

1850 AD to 1860 AD

Industrial Revolution

1860 AD to 1870 AD

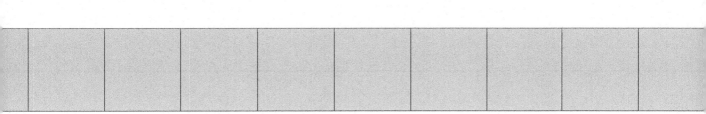

Industrial Revolution

1870 AD to 1880 AD

Industrial Revolution

1880 AD to 1890 AD

Industrial Revolution
1890 AD to 1900 AD

The Modern World
1900 AD to 1905 AD

The Modern World
1905 AD to 1910 AD

The Modern World
1910 AD to 1915 AD

The Modern World
1915 AD to 1920 AD

The Modern World
1920 AD to 1925 AD

The Modern World

1925 AD to 1930 AD

The Modern World
1930 AD to 1935 AD

The Modern World
1935 AD to 1940 AD

The Modern World
1940 AD to 1945 AD

The Modern World
1945 AD to 1950 AD

The Modern World
1950 AD to 1955 AD

The Modern World
1955 AD to 1960 AD

The Modern World
1960 AD to 1965 AD

The Modern World
1965 AD to 1970 AD

The Modern World
1970 AD to 1975 AD

The Modern World
1975 AD to 1980 AD

The Modern World
1980 AD to 1985 AD

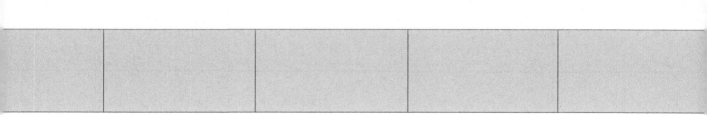

The Modern World
1985 AD to 1990 AD

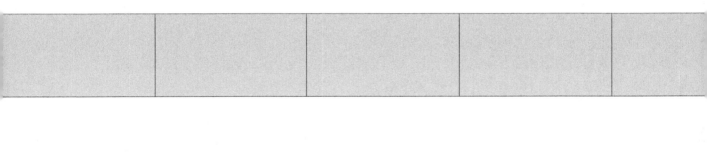

The Modern World
1990 AD to 1995 AD

The Modern World

1995 AD to 2000 AD

MODERN

The Modern World
2000 AD to 2005 AD

The Modern World

2005 AD to 2010 AD

The Modern World
2010 AD to 2015 AD

The Modern World
2015 AD to 2020 AD

The Modern World
2020 AD to 2025 AD

The Modern World
2025 AD to 2030 AD

The Modern World
2030 AD to 2035 AD

The Modern World
2035 AD to 2040 AD

The Modern World
2040 AD to 2045 AD

The Modern World
2045 AD to 2050 AD

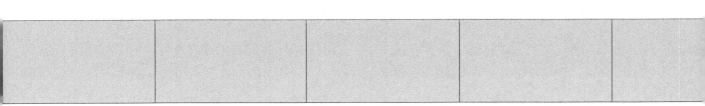

The Modern World
2050 AD to 2055 AD

The Modern World
2055 AD to 2060 AD

Made in the USA
Las Vegas, NV
21 May 2022